To Paul,
Oscar & Lara.

In the run up to Christmas of 2019, the family talked about **gifts** on which they were keen.

The parents felt **strongly** that their kids had enough and wanted a change from simply more **stuff**.

An idea was born about rescuing a **kitten,**
which was warmly received by the kids who were smitten.

Yet the idea of just one immediately **grew,**

to an obvious response
that they must find
two.

The **Dad** of the family was not wholly on board,
but a trip to the shelter close by was soon scored,
on arrival they discovered six **kittens** in need,
of varying colours and who knows what breed.

Five were so tiny, so visibly small,
but one was quite obviously the **largest** of all,

the largest, they said, had had three homes fall through,
the boy of the family said well then **'I'd like you'**.

The boy had a large heart, so pure and so kind,
the staff were surprised but he'd made up his mind,
he was quite certain, the ball of **ginger** and **white,**
was to be his at almost first sight.

The girl of the family found it so hard to choose, but the little grey boy remained first in the queue, so the two were selected, the **ginger** and **grey** and the SPCA checked their home the next day.

The home visit went well, indeed all was approved,

the two kittens were cleared to be ready to move.

They both needed names, the children were ready,

they decided quite quickly on **Lion** and **Teddy.**

A point yet to mention, but one you should know,
the family already had **two dogs** in tow.

Bemused were the dogs, both Jackson and Bentley,

yet they amazingly welcomed the kittens so gently.

Lion and Teddy were **hugged** beyond measure,
every day was **exciting,** they provided such pleasure,
a toy wrapped in paper, a traditional sight,
could never provide so much laughter and light.

Christmas was memorable
especially the **tree,**
as Lion soon realised she could
climb it with glee,
what wonderful gifts for the
family of four,
two new additions for them to
adore.

As the new year arrived the outdoors was calling,
the children were anxious of hazards and falling,
but these two adventurers were not to be tamed,
in fact in the neighbourhood
they soon became **famed.**

Lion was often found in the **rain,**

out at all hours, once found in a **drain.**

Teddy, at times, was more like a **dog,**

chasing after the children, even joining their jog.

Other **cats** in the area could often be found,
at the back of the house on some shared open ground,
the kittens soon realised that this was the place,
to meet up with new **friends** and find their own space.

One day Teddy returned, his **collar** was gone,
the children went looking and searched on and on,
a new collar was bought and put on his neck,
which the family thought would keep him **in check.**

Three days later, that week, when
Lion came home,
her collar was gone with her name
tag in chrome.

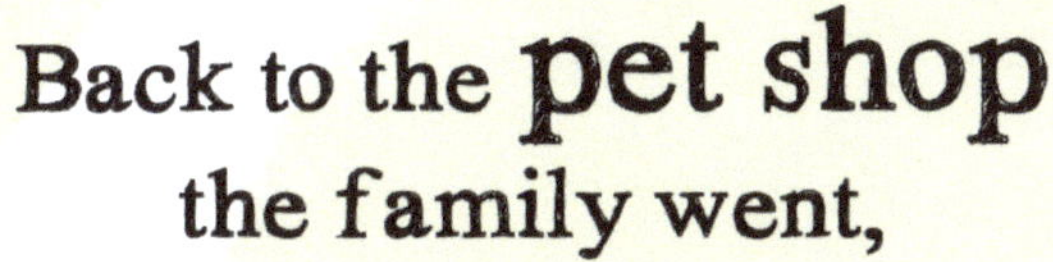
Back to the **pet shop**
the family went,

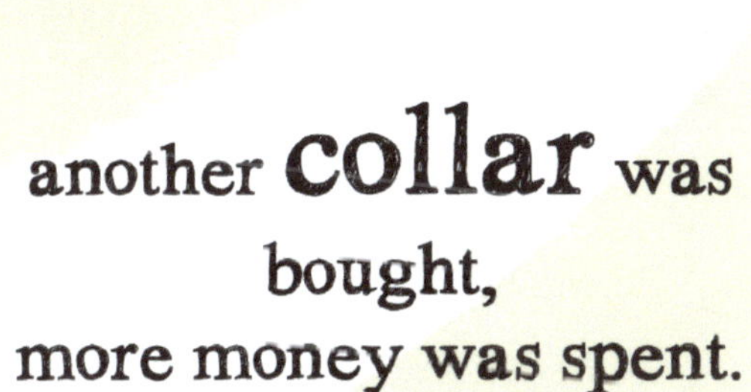
another **collar** was
bought,
more money was spent.

Seven collars went missing by the end of month two, they considered a technique using very strong glue.

Then one day a
gardener from
somewhere close by,
returned one of the
collars from a tree, right
up high.

The family discussed where
the collars could be,

the children told stories and **giggled** with glee,
they just couldn't fathom how so many were lost
and wondered if the collars made the kittens feel cross.

Here are some stories made up round the table,
maybe one collar is hooked on a cable,

another is tangled
in reeds in a
stream,

or floating in
liquid, possibly
cream.

Maybe there's one on a **swing** in a playground,

or attached to a **gate**

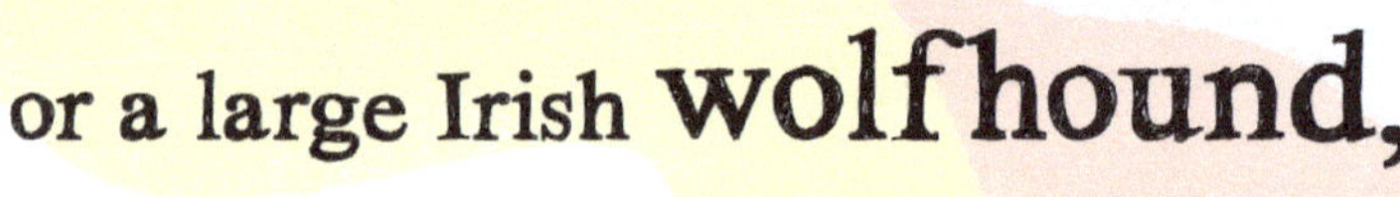

or a large Irish **wolfhound,**

or one caught on a table cloth edged with white lace.

Buying **new collars** from all over town,
became part of routine, not producing a frown,

they were added as standard to the weekly **food list**, spare collars were necessary and could not be missed.

Remember the father who was mentioned before,

he became a **cat lover,** right down to his core.

It's good to remember how love can just start, and before you quite know it, take over your **heart.**

The **kittens** were simply the best ever decision,
fulfilling Christmas's joy, its spirit and vision,
when next Christmas arrives maybe you could ponder,
on a **rescue** like this that fills lives with such wonder.

Author: Kelly Myatt
Illustrator: Amber Walsh

First published in South Africa 2024 by Nuñez Books.

ISBN: 978-1-0370-1051-4
Contact us:
info@kellymyatt.com
ambiewalsh22@gmail.com
Instagram:
@kelly_myatt
@amberwalshart

www.ingramcontent.com/pod-product-compliance
Lightning Source LLC
LaVergne TN
LVHW071223160826
845679LV00003B/893

* 9 7 8 1 0 3 7 0 1 0 5 1 4 *